# Mental Maths Every Day
## for ages 9–10

Dear Parents,

Thank you for buying this copy of *Mental Maths Every Day 9–10*, one of a six book series of maths practice books for primary aged children.

*Why is mental maths so important?*
All children need to know number facts so that they can remember them instantly when working on more complex aspects of maths. Children who are confident in mental maths also tend to be more confident when faced with money, time, measurements and other mathematical concepts.

This book is designed to boost children's confidence by giving them plenty of practice in quick calculations. The calculations become progressively more difficult as the child works through the book. Don't be surprised if the first few pages seem easy – it's still important that your child completes them. Your child will find some of the other pages very difficult but this is quite normal too; just be on hand to provide help and guidance when needed.

*How do I use the book?*
Each page of this book is split into columns of questions that have been specially devised for children aged 9–10. Using a stopwatch or clock, ask your child to do as many questions as possible from the first column in exactly one minute. Allow your child to use fingers or counters if she/he needs to. Prompt your child to look very carefully at each question, paying special attention to the mathematical symbol – for example, whether it is an instruction to add or subtract.

At the end of the minute, mark the questions with your child and write down the score for the column in the score box. To save time, the answers are provided on pages 30 to 32. Your child probably won't have time to complete all the questions in the column but praise her/him for trying hard and doing as many as possible. Take the opportunity to discuss any mistakes that have been made and show the child how to do any questions that have been missed out. When she/he is ready your child can complete the next column and try and improve the score. Don't worry if it doesn't improve immediately – 'practice makes perfect' and the improvement in performance will take place sooner or later. Remember that the best way to help is to give lots of praise for success and lots of support where the child is experiencing any difficulty. I do hope that your child enjoys working through the activities.

Andrew Brodie

# Contents

# Adding numbers up to 30

See if you can answer each set of 20 questions in one minute.

**Column 1**

7 + 9 =

12 + 13 =

2 + 18 =

9 + 4 =

14 + 7 =

1 + 23 =

3 + 12 =

16 + 8 =

11 + 5 =

5 + 17 =

20 + 4 =

15 + 13 =

4 + 7 =

10 + 18 =

6 + 15 =

8 + 16 =

13 + 7 =

3 + 6 =

8 + 7 =

4 + 12 =

Score

**Column 2**

17 + 8 =

16 + 5 =

14 + 9 =

6 + 23 =

2 + 19 =

9 + 12 =

12 + 18 =

5 + 16 =

7 + 17 =

10 + 14 =

3 + 25 =

11 + 19 =

15 + 12 =

7 + 14 =

8 + 9 =

17 + 5 =

11 + 16 =

4 + 22 =

19 + 8 =

13 + 16 =

Score

**Column 3**

20 + 7 =

15 + 9 =

4 + 17 =

10 + 11 =

6 + 17 =

7 + 8 =

5 + 14 =

9 + 13 =

14 + 13 =

1 + 26 =

3 + 18 =

4 + 9 =

8 + 21 =

13 + 9 =

12 + 17 =

3 + 19 =

8 + 14 =

2 + 8 =

16 + 4 =

11 + 8 =

Score

**Column 4**

21 + 8 =

14 + 12 =

17 + 9 =

6 + 18 =

10 + 17 =

5 + 23 =

24 + 4 =

4 + 18 =

18 + 11 =

15 + 8 =

9 + 7 =

18 + 6 =

11 + 9 =

9 + 19 =

13 + 8 =

15 + 7 =

19 + 6 =

6 + 21 =

9 + 16 =

8 + 18 =

Score

For answers see page 30

See if you can answer each set of 20 questions in one minute.

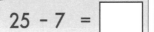

| | | | |
|---|---|---|---|
| 25 − 7 = | 27 − 13 = | 19 − 13 = | 26 − 15 = |
| 14 − 6 = | 25 − 8 = | 24 − 8 = | 25 − 9 = |
| 21 − 8 = | 19 − 6 = | 21 − 9 = | 17 − 11 = |
| 24 − 12 = | 30 − 16 = | 21 − 15 = | 23 − 21 = |
| 15 − 9 = | 26 − 17 = | 14 − 12 = | 19 − 7 = |
| 27 − 8 = | 21 − 7 = | 28 − 17 = | 16 − 9 = |
| 19 − 14 = | 29 − 8 = | 16 − 8 = | 21 − 17 = |
| 26 − 18 = | 23 − 5 = | 17 − 9 = | 12 − 9 = |
| 22 − 9 = | 12 − 7 = | 22 − 13 = | 25 − 25 = |
| 18 − 13 = | 22 − 15 = | 18 − 15 = | 20 − 14 = |
| 20 − 13 = | 24 − 9 = | 27 − 15 = | 15 − 8 = |
| 28 − 23 = | 28 − 5 = | 15 − 11 = | 29 − 24 = |
| 16 − 14 = | 20 − 15 = | 29 − 5 = | 18 − 11 = |
| 13 − 9 = | 13 − 11 = | 23 − 12 = | 26 − 22 = |
| 30 − 18 = | 26 − 9 = | 13 − 8 = | 17 − 13 = |
| 23 − 7 = | 18 − 12 = | 24 − 18 = | 21 − 18 = |
| 17 − 15 = | 15 − 7 = | 20 − 12 = | 28 − 25 = |
| 29 − 16 = | 27 − 6 = | 14 − 9 = | 18 − 6 = |
| 16 − 7 = | 17 − 5 = | 11 − 7 = | 22 − 16 = |
| 25 − 14 = | 23 − 9 = | 30 − 24 = | 27 − 14 = |
| Score | Score | Score | Score |

# Adding and subtraction up to 30

See if you can answer each set of 20 questions in one minute.

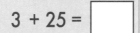

| | | | |
|---|---|---|---|
| 3 + 25 = | 4 + 22 = | 27 – 14 = | 23 – 12 = |
| 25 – 9 = | 15 – 9 = | 10 + 14 = | 9 + 19 = |
| 27 – 15 = | 15 + 9 = | 26 – 18 = | 17 – 5 = |
| 12 + 17 = | 19 – 7 = | 4 + 9 = | 1 + 23 = |
| 15 – 11 = | 6 + 18 = | 13 – 11 = | 26 – 15 = |
| 3 + 19 = | 29 – 5 = | 4 + 7 = | 9 + 13 = |
| 18 + 11 = | 12 – 7 = | 22 – 15 = | 17 – 9 = |
| 17 – 11 = | 5 + 16 = | 18 – 6 = | 30 – 24 = |
| 6 + 15 = | 7 + 8 = | 7 + 17 = | 20 + 4 = |
| 23 – 5 = | 21 – 7 = | 21 – 18 = | 21 – 17 = |
| 9 + 12 = | 7 + 9 = | 18 + 6 = | 24 – 9 = |
| 14 – 6 = | 24 – 12 = | 22 – 16 = | 15 + 13 = |
| 10 + 17 = | 6 + 21 = | 9 + 4 = | 19 – 14 = |
| 5 + 23 = | 19 + 8 = | 20 – 15 = | 9 + 7 = |
| 18 – 15 = | 29 – 8 = | 27 – 8 = | 13 + 8 = |
| 12 + 18 = | 5 + 17 = | 11 + 9 = | 28 – 25 = |
| 25 – 7 = | 11 – 7 = | 21 – 8 = | 8 + 21 = |
| 4 + 17 = | 2 + 19 = | 14 + 7 = | 16 – 9 = |
| 23 – 21 = | 11 + 5 = | 26 – 9 = | 15 + 7 = |
| 12 + 13 = | 28 – 5 = | 14 + 9 = | 22 – 13 = |
| Score | Score | Score | Score |

# The 2 times table

See if you can answer each set of 20 questions in one minute.

| Column 1 | Column 2 | Column 3 | Column 4 |
|---|---|---|---|
| $0 \times 2 =$ | $4 \times 2 =$ | $6 \times 2 =$ | $8 \times 2 =$ |
| $1 \times 2 =$ | $8 \times 2 =$ | $8 \times 2 =$ | $3 \times 2 =$ |
| $2 \times 2 =$ | $0 \times 2 =$ | $2 \times 2 =$ | $0 \times 2 =$ |
| $3 \times 2 =$ | $10 \times 2 =$ | $10 \times 2 =$ | $10 \times 2 =$ |
| $4 \times 2 =$ | $6 \times 2 =$ | $1 \times 2 =$ | $9 \times 2 =$ |
| $5 \times 2 =$ | $2 \times 2 =$ | $5 \times 2 =$ | $5 \times 2 =$ |
| $6 \times 2 =$ | $9 \times 2 =$ | $0 \times 2 =$ | $7 \times 2 =$ |
| $7 \times 2 =$ | $3 \times 2 =$ | $3 \times 2 =$ | $2 \times 2 =$ |
| $8 \times 2 =$ | $1 \times 2 =$ | $4 \times 2 =$ | $4 \times 2 =$ |
| $9 \times 2 =$ | $5 \times 2 =$ | $7 \times 2 =$ | $1 \times 2 =$ |
| $10 \times 2 =$ | $7 \times 2 =$ | $9 \times 2 =$ | $6 \times 2 =$ |
| $18 \div 2 =$ | $16 \div 2 =$ | $12 \div 2 =$ | $20 \div 2 =$ |
| $10 \div 2 =$ | $2 \div 2 =$ | $6 \div 2 =$ | $18 \div 2 =$ |
| $4 \div 2 =$ | $12 \div 2 =$ | $4 \div 2 =$ | $2 \div 2 =$ |
| $6 \div 2 =$ | $20 \div 2 =$ | $10 \div 2 =$ | $8 \div 2 =$ |
| $14 \div 2 =$ | $6 \div 2 =$ | $2 \div 2 =$ | $4 \div 2 =$ |
| $8 \div 2 =$ | $4 \div 2 =$ | $8 \div 2 =$ | $10 \div 2 =$ |
| $2 \div 2 =$ | $18 \div 2 =$ | $18 \div 2 =$ | $14 \div 2 =$ |
| $20 \div 2 =$ | $8 \div 2 =$ | $16 \div 2 =$ | $6 \div 2 =$ |
| $16 \div 2 =$ | $14 \div 2 =$ | $14 \div 2 =$ | $16 \div 2 =$ |
| Score | Score | Score | Score |

For answers see page 30

See if you can answer each set of 20 questions in one minute.

| | | | |
|---|---|---|---|
| 0 × 3 = | 5 × 3 = | 4 × 3 = | 8 × 3 = |
| 1 × 3 = | 8 × 3 = | 1 × 3 = | 2 × 3 = |
| 2 × 3 = | 10 × 3 = | 9 × 3 = | 9 × 3 = |
| 3 × 3 = | 2 × 3 = | 5 × 3 = | 0 × 3 = |
| 4 × 3 = | 6 × 3 = | 6 × 3 = | 6 × 3 = |
| 5 × 3 = | 7 × 3 = | 10 × 3 = | 1 × 3 = |
| 6 × 3 = | 9 × 3 = | 8 × 3 = | 4 × 3 = |
| 7 × 3 = | 0 × 3 = | 2 × 3 = | 10 × 3 = |
| 8 × 3 = | 4 × 3 = | 0 × 3 = | 3 × 3 = |
| 9 × 3 = | 1 × 3 = | 7 × 3 = | 5 × 3 = |
| 10 × 3 = | 3 × 3 = | 3 × 3 = | 7 × 3 = |
| 24 ÷ 3 = | 24 ÷ 3 = | 30 ÷ 3 = | 15 ÷ 3 = |
| 15 ÷ 3 = | 15 ÷ 3 = | 24 ÷ 3 = | 27 ÷ 3 = |
| 18 ÷ 3 = | 9 ÷ 3 = | 3 ÷ 3 = | 6 ÷ 3 = |
| 9 ÷ 3 = | 3 ÷ 3 = | 15 ÷ 3 = | 3 ÷ 3 = |
| 30 ÷ 3 = | 30 ÷ 3 = | 9 ÷ 3 = | 12 ÷ 3 = |
| 6 ÷ 3 = | 21 ÷ 3 = | 6 ÷ 3 = | 30 ÷ 3 = |
| 12 ÷ 3 = | 6 ÷ 3 = | 18 ÷ 3 = | 24 ÷ 3 = |
| 27 ÷ 3 = | 27 ÷ 3 = | 12 ÷ 3 = | 9 ÷ 3 = |
| 3 ÷ 3 = | 18 ÷ 3 = | 21 ÷ 3 = | 18 ÷ 3 = |
| Score | Score | Score | Score |

For answers see page 30

# Adding one-digit numbers to two-digit numbers

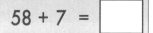

See if you can answer each set of 20 questions in one minute.

| | | | |
|---|---|---|---|
| 58 + 7 = | 48 + 3 = | 79 + 2 = | 18 + 7 = |
| 27 + 4 = | 64 + 9 = | 68 + 4 = | 47 + 4 = |
| 68 + 8 = | 35 + 6 = | 29 + 5 = | 58 + 8 = |
| 75 + 6 = | 23 + 9 = | 48 + 3 = | 35 + 6 = |
| 59 + 6 = | 57 + 4 = | 35 + 9 = | 68 + 5 = |
| 82 + 9 = | 82 + 9 = | 46 + 8 = | 42 + 9 = |
| 36 + 5 = | 87 + 4 = | 24 + 7 = | 64 + 7 = |
| 49 + 2 = | 38 + 5 = | 59 + 2 = | 76 + 5 = |
| 68 + 4 = | 42 + 9 = | 68 + 6 = | 58 + 6 = |
| 73 + 8 = | 58 + 6 = | 36 + 6 = | 34 + 7 = |
| 55 + 7 = | 29 + 2 = | 88 + 8 = | 37 + 4 = |
| 88 + 3 = | 67 + 5 = | 59 + 2 = | 22 + 9 = |
| 28 + 5 = | 26 + 5 = | 78 + 4 = | 17 + 5 = |
| 64 + 7 = | 14 + 7 = | 19 + 3 = | 79 + 2 = |
| 87 + 4 = | 26 + 8 = | 26 + 5 = | 47 + 5 = |
| 22 + 9 = | 55 + 9 = | 34 + 9 = | 79 + 6 = |
| 17 + 5 = | 66 + 6 = | 45 + 6 = | 22 + 9 = |
| 68 + 6 = | 22 + 9 = | 67 + 5 = | 66 + 5 = |
| 35 + 6 = | 85 + 8 = | 89 + 2 = | 59 + 2 = |
| 18 + 5 = | 38 + 7 = | 24 + 8 = | 34 + 8 = |
| Score | Score | Score | Score |

For answers see page 30

# The 4 times table

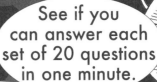See if you can answer each set of 20 questions in one minute.

| | | | |
|---|---|---|---|
| 0 × 4 = | 4 × 4 = | 9 × 4 = | 2 × 4 = |
| 1 × 4 = | 0 × 4 = | 1 × 4 = | 7 × 4 = |
| 2 × 4 = | 7 × 4 = | 3 × 4 = | 10 × 4 = |
| 3 × 4 = | 5 × 4 = | 6 × 4 = | 3 × 4 = |
| 4 × 4 = | 10 × 4 = | 5 × 4 = | 1 × 4 = |
| 5 × 4 = | 8 × 4 = | 4 × 4 = | 6 × 4 = |
| 6 × 4 = | 1 × 4 = | 0 × 4 = | 9 × 4 = |
| 7 × 4 = | 3 × 4 = | 10 × 4 = | 5 × 4 = |
| 8 × 4 = | 9 × 4 = | 2 × 4 = | 8 × 4 = |
| 9 × 4 = | 2 × 4 = | 8 × 4 = | 4 × 4 = |
| 10 × 4 = | 6 × 4 = | 7 × 4 = | 0 × 4 = |
| 36 ÷ 4 = | 4 ÷ 4 = | 20 ÷ 4 = | 40 ÷ 4 = |
| 12 ÷ 4 = | 16 ÷ 4 = | 28 ÷ 4 = | 12 ÷ 4 = |
| 8 ÷ 4 = | 24 ÷ 4 = | 16 ÷ 4 = | 4 ÷ 4 = |
| 40 ÷ 4 = | 32 ÷ 4 = | 8 ÷ 4 = | 36 ÷ 4 = |
| 32 ÷ 4 = | 40 ÷ 4 = | 24 ÷ 4 = | 8 ÷ 4 = |
| 16 ÷ 4 = | 8 ÷ 4 = | 4 ÷ 4 = | 24 ÷ 4 = |
| 4 ÷ 4 = | 28 ÷ 4 = | 40 ÷ 4 = | 16 ÷ 4 = |
| 24 ÷ 4 = | 36 ÷ 4 = | 36 ÷ 4 = | 28 ÷ 4 = |
| 20 ÷ 4 = | 20 ÷ 4 = | 32 ÷ 4 = | 20 ÷ 4 = |
| Score | Score | Score | Score |

For answers see page 30

# Subtracting one-digit numbers from two-digit numbers

See if you can answer each set of 20 questions in one minute.

| | | | |
|---|---|---|---|
| 92 − 6 = | 54 − 5 = | 65 − 7 = | 23 − 9 = |
| 81 − 8 = | 42 − 5 = | 34 − 5 = | 61 − 4 = |
| 71 − 4 = | 82 − 5 = | 71 − 3 = | 44 − 5 = |
| 51 − 4 = | 63 − 7 = | 45 − 8 = | 84 − 6 = |
| 12 − 7 = | 78 − 9 = | 78 − 9 = | 72 − 6 = |
| 33 − 9 = | 21 − 2 = | 35 − 6 = | 95 − 9 = |
| 46 − 8 = | 65 − 7 = | 42 − 6 = | 62 − 8 = |
| 57 − 8 = | 33 − 8 = | 55 − 8 = | 25 − 7 = |
| 84 − 5 = | 86 − 7 = | 82 − 3 = | 45 − 8 = |
| 77 − 9 = | 44 − 9 = | 56 − 9 = | 71 − 2 = |
| 31 − 3 = | 52 − 4 = | 44 − 7 = | 53 − 4 = |
| 66 − 8 = | 24 − 6 = | 31 − 6 = | 38 − 9 = |
| 74 − 8 = | 81 − 5 = | 64 − 5 = | 24 − 5 = |
| 32 − 5 = | 72 − 3 = | 73 − 8 = | 61 − 7 = |
| 45 − 7 = | 85 − 9 = | 41 − 5 = | 84 − 5 = |
| 63 − 9 = | 45 − 7 = | 65 − 8 = | 48 − 9 = |
| 46 − 8 = | 73 − 7 = | 72 − 6 = | 62 − 3 = |
| 21 − 4 = | 88 − 9 = | 34 − 5 = | 77 − 9 = |
| 32 − 7 = | 25 − 6 = | 25 − 7 = | 31 − 2 = |
| 34 − 9 = | 46 − 9 = | 65 − 6 = | 52 − 5 = |
| Score | Score | Score | Score |

For answers see page 30

# The 5 times table

See if you can answer each set of 20 questions in one minute.

| | | | |
|---|---|---|---|
| 0 × 5 = | 2 × 5 = | 7 × 5 = | 0 × 5 = |
| 1 × 5 = | 6 × 5 = | 0 × 5 = | 8 × 5 = |
| 2 × 5 = | 9 × 5 = | 4 × 5 = | 5 × 5 = |
| 3 × 5 = | 10 × 5 = | 1 × 5 = | 3 × 5 = |
| 4 × 5 = | 0 × 5 = | 9 × 5 = | 1 × 5 = |
| 5 × 5 = | 3 × 5 = | 5 × 5 = | 10 × 5 = |
| 6 × 5 = | 8 × 5 = | 3 × 5 = | 2 × 5 = |
| 7 × 5 = | 4 × 5 = | 6 × 5 = | 4 × 5 = |
| 8 × 5 = | 1 × 5 = | 10 × 5 = | 6 × 5 = |
| 9 × 5 = | 5 × 5 = | 8 × 5 = | 9 × 5 = |
| 10 × 5 = | 7 × 5 = | 2 × 5 = | 7 × 5 = |
| 40 ÷ 5 = | 50 ÷ 5 = | 10 ÷ 5 = | 5 ÷ 5 = |
| 20 ÷ 5 = | 30 ÷ 5 = | 35 ÷ 5 = | 15 ÷ 5 = |
| 5 ÷ 5 = | 45 ÷ 5 = | 25 ÷ 5 = | 50 ÷ 5 = |
| 15 ÷ 5 = | 25 ÷ 5 = | 20 ÷ 5 = | 25 ÷ 5 = |
| 50 ÷ 5 = | 10 ÷ 5 = | 40 ÷ 5 = | 30 ÷ 5 = |
| 45 ÷ 5 = | 5 ÷ 5 = | 50 ÷ 5 = | 10 ÷ 5 = |
| 10 ÷ 5 = | 15 ÷ 5 = | 5 ÷ 5 = | 40 ÷ 5 = |
| 35 ÷ 5 = | 35 ÷ 5 = | 30 ÷ 5 = | 20 ÷ 5 = |
| 30 ÷ 5 = | 20 ÷ 5 = | 45 ÷ 5 = | 45 ÷ 5 = |
| Score | Score | Score | Score |

For answers see page 30

# Finding halves of even numbers

See if you can answer each set of 20 questions in one minute.

| | | | |
|---|---|---|---|
| half of 48 = | half of 72 = | half of 74 = | half of 36 = |
| half of 70 = | half of 34 = | half of 88 = | half of 24 = |
| half of 24 = | half of 88 = | half of 64 = | half of 48 = |
| half of 12 = | half of 46 = | half of 28 = | half of 50 = |
| half of 34 = | half of 58 = | half of 52 = | half of 32 = |
| half of 66 = | half of 22 = | half of 34 = | half of 94 = |
| half of 52 = | half of 48 = | half of 22 = | half of 64 = |
| half of 64 = | half of 98 = | half of 16 = | half of 88 = |
| half of 18 = | half of 76 = | half of 78 = | half of 30 = |
| half of 74 = | half of 42 = | half of 94 = | half of 42 = |
| half of 42 = | half of 52 = | half of 46 = | half of 62 = |
| half of 86 = | half of 36 = | half of 58 = | half of 54 = |
| half of 36 = | half of 66 = | half of 10 = | half of 44 = |
| half of 58 = | half of 14 = | half of 24 = | half of 86 = |
| half of 68 = | half of 64 = | half of 84 = | half of 38 = |
| half of 14 = | half of 54 = | half of 44 = | half of 10 = |
| half of 46 = | half of 96 = | half of 52 = | half of 66 = |
| half of 50 = | half of 60 = | half of 40 = | half of 84 = |
| half of 22 = | half of 38 = | half of 56 = | half of 96 = |
| half of 40 = | half of 18 = | half of 94 = | half of 52 = |
| Score | Score | Score | Score |

For answers see page 31

# The 6 times table

See if you can answer each set of 20 questions in one minute.

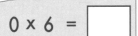

| | | | |
|---|---|---|---|
| 0 × 6 = | 2 × 6 = | 5 × 6 = | 1 × 6 = |
| 1 × 6 = | 7 × 6 = | 1 × 6 = | 9 × 6 = |
| 2 × 6 = | 0 × 6 = | 10 × 6 = | 4 × 6 = |
| 3 × 6 = | 10 × 6 = | 8 × 6 = | 2 × 6 = |
| 4 × 6 = | 3 × 6 = | 4 × 6 = | 5 × 6 = |
| 5 × 6 = | 4 × 6 = | 3 × 6 = | 7 × 6 = |
| 6 × 6 = | 9 × 6 = | 9 × 6 = | 0 × 6 = |
| 7 × 6 = | 1 × 6 = | 6 × 6 = | 3 × 6 = |
| 8 × 6 = | 5 × 6 = | 2 × 6 = | 8 × 6 = |
| 9 × 6 = | 8 × 6 = | 0 × 6 = | 10 × 6 = |
| 10 × 6 = | 6 × 6 = | 7 × 6 = | 6 × 6 = |
| 48 ÷ 6 = | 60 ÷ 6 = | 6 ÷ 6 = | 54 ÷ 6 = |
| 60 ÷ 6 = | 42 ÷ 6 = | 36 ÷ 6 = | 42 ÷ 6 = |
| 12 ÷ 6 = | 24 ÷ 6 = | 48 ÷ 6 = | 12 ÷ 6 = |
| 30 ÷ 6 = | 18 ÷ 6 = | 60 ÷ 6 = | 30 ÷ 6 = |
| 6 ÷ 6 = | 6 ÷ 6 = | 42 ÷ 6 = | 60 ÷ 6 = |
| 42 ÷ 6 = | 30 ÷ 6 = | 30 ÷ 6 = | 18 ÷ 6 = |
| 24 ÷ 6 = | 48 ÷ 6 = | 54 ÷ 6 = | 36 ÷ 6 = |
| 18 ÷ 6 = | 12 ÷ 6 = | 24 ÷ 6 = | 6 ÷ 6 = |
| 54 ÷ 6 = | 36 ÷ 6 = | 18 ÷ 6 = | 48 ÷ 6 = |
| Score | Score | Score | Score |

For answers see page 31

# Finding halves of odd numbers

See if you can answer each set of 15 questions in one minute.

| | | | |
|---|---|---|---|
| half of 17 = | half of 77 = | half of 3 = | half of 85 = |
| half of 41 = | half of 87 = | half of 57 = | half of 47 = |
| half of 7 = | half of 21 = | half of 73 = | half of 11 = |
| half of 23 = | half of 27 = | half of 91 = | half of 43 = |
| half of 95 = | half of 49 = | half of 75 = | half of 97 = |
| half of 55 = | half of 63 = | half of 15 = | half of 17 = |
| half of 79 = | half of 37 = | half of 65 = | half of 19 = |
| half of 19 = | half of 53 = | half of 51 = | half of 27 = |
| half of 83 = | half of 71 = | half of 13 = | half of 67 = |
| half of 5 = | half of 25 = | half of 81 = | half of 59 = |
| half of 99 = | half of 33 = | half of 25 = | half of 73 = |
| half of 47 = | half of 29 = | half of 35 = | half of 31 = |
| half of 85 = | half of 69 = | half of 89 = | half of 63 = |
| half of 45 = | half of 59 = | half of 39 = | half of 7 = |
| half of 31 = | half of 21 = | half of 19 = | half of 9 = |
| Score | Score | Score | Score |

For answers see page 31

# The 7 times table

See if you can answer each set of 20 questions in one minute.

| | | | |
|---|---|---|---|
| 0 x 7 = | 2 x 7 = | 5 x 7 = | 4 x 7 = |
| 1 x 7 = | 5 x 7 = | 9 x 7 = | 1 x 7 = |
| 2 x 7 = | 9 x 7 = | 0 x 7 = | 10 x 7 = |
| 3 x 7 = | 0 x 7 = | 4 x 7 = | 2 x 7 = |
| 4 x 7 = | 6 x 7 = | 2 x 7 = | 9 x 7 = |
| 5 x 7 = | 3 x 7 = | 6 x 7 = | 7 x 7 = |
| 6 x 7 = | 1 x 7 = | 1 x 7 = | 3 x 7 = |
| 7 x 7 = | 10 x 7 = | 3 x 7 = | 0 x 7 = |
| 8 x 7 = | 8 x 7 = | 10 x 7 = | 5 x 7 = |
| 9 x 7 = | 4 x 7 = | 7 x 7 = | 8 x 7 = |
| 10 x 7 = | 7 x 7 = | 8 x 7 = | 6 x 7 = |
| 49 ÷ 7 = | 14 ÷ 7 = | 42 ÷ 7 = | 70 ÷ 7 = |
| 42 ÷ 7 = | 28 ÷ 7 = | 63 ÷ 7 = | 35 ÷ 7 = |
| 56 ÷ 7 = | 7 ÷ 7 = | 7 ÷ 7 = | 56 ÷ 7 = |
| 7 ÷ 7 = | 70 ÷ 7 = | 35 ÷ 7 = | 14 ÷ 7 = |
| 35 ÷ 7 = | 56 ÷ 7 = | 49 ÷ 7 = | 49 ÷ 7 = |
| 70 ÷ 7 = | 21 ÷ 7 = | 14 ÷ 7 = | 21 ÷ 7 = |
| 28 ÷ 7 = | 35 ÷ 7 = | 70 ÷ 7 = | 42 ÷ 7 = |
| 21 ÷ 7 = | 42 ÷ 7 = | 56 ÷ 7 = | 7 ÷ 7 = |
| 14 ÷ 7 = | 49 ÷ 7 = | 28 ÷ 7 = | 28 ÷ 7 = |
| Score | Score | Score | Score |

# Finding quarters

See if you can answer each set of 15 questions in one minute.

quarter of 12 = ☐

quarter of 88 = ☐

quarter of 60 = ☐

quarter of 36 = ☐

quarter of 40 = ☐

quarter of 32 = ☐

quarter of 64 = ☐

quarter of 16 = ☐

quarter of 4 = ☐

quarter of 20 = ☐

quarter of 56 = ☐

quarter of 84 = ☐

quarter of 24 = ☐

quarter of 28 = ☐

quarter of 52 = ☐

Score ☐

quarter of 20 = ☐

quarter of 16 = ☐

quarter of 44 = ☐

quarter of 68 = ☐

quarter of 8 = ☐

quarter of 84 = ☐

quarter of 100 = ☐

quarter of 40 = ☐

quarter of 24 = ☐

quarter of 88 = ☐

quarter of 36 = ☐

quarter of 28 = ☐

quarter of 12 = ☐

quarter of 48 = ☐

quarter of 72 = ☐

Score ☐

quarter of 16 = ☐

quarter of 80 = ☐

quarter of 24 = ☐

quarter of 32 = ☐

quarter of 56 = ☐

quarter of 72 = ☐

quarter of 8 = ☐

quarter of 28 = ☐

quarter of 36 = ☐

quarter of 4 = ☐

quarter of 12 = ☐

quarter of 40 = ☐

quarter of 8 = ☐

quarter of 60 = ☐

quarter of 20 = ☐

Score ☐

quarter of 24 = ☐

quarter of 8 = ☐

quarter of 44 = ☐

quarter of 28 = ☐

quarter of 40 = ☐

quarter of 100 = ☐

quarter of 64 = ☐

quarter of 12 = ☐

quarter of 84 = ☐

quarter of 76 = ☐

quarter of 48 = ☐

quarter of 60 = ☐

quarter of 12 = ☐

quarter of 16 = ☐

quarter of 20 = ☐

Score ☐

For answers see page 31

# The 8 times table

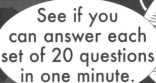 See if you can answer each set of 20 questions in one minute.

| | | | |
|---|---|---|---|
| 0 × 8 = | 2 × 8 = | 5 × 8 = | 9 × 8 = |
| 1 × 8 = | 10 × 8 = | 3 × 8 = | 2 × 8 = |
| 2 × 8 = | 3 × 8 = | 1 × 8 = | 5 × 8 = |
| 3 × 8 = | 7 × 8 = | 6 × 8 = | 10 × 8 = |
| 4 × 8 = | 6 × 8 = | 0 × 8 = | 3 × 8 = |
| 5 × 8 = | 4 × 8 = | 4 × 8 = | 1 × 8 = |
| 6 × 8 = | 9 × 8 = | 8 × 8 = | 4 × 8 = |
| 7 × 8 = | 1 × 8 = | 2 × 8 = | 8 × 8 = |
| 8 × 8 = | 8 × 8 = | 10 × 8 = | 0 × 8 = |
| 9 × 8 = | 0 × 8 = | 7 × 8 = | 6 × 8 = |
| 10 × 8 = | 5 × 8 = | 9 × 8 = | 7 × 8 = |
| 64 ÷ 8 = | 8 ÷ 8 = | 32 ÷ 8 = | 64 ÷ 8 = |
| 8 ÷ 8 = | 40 ÷ 8 = | 80 ÷ 8 = | 16 ÷ 8 = |
| 16 ÷ 8 = | 80 ÷ 8 = | 56 ÷ 8 = | 56 ÷ 8 = |
| 40 ÷ 8 = | 24 ÷ 8 = | 40 ÷ 8 = | 8 ÷ 8 = |
| 24 ÷ 8 = | 32 ÷ 8 = | 48 ÷ 8 = | 80 ÷ 8 = |
| 72 ÷ 8 = | 64 ÷ 8 = | 24 ÷ 8 = | 24 ÷ 8 = |
| 48 ÷ 8 = | 48 ÷ 8 = | 72 ÷ 8 = | 48 ÷ 8 = |
| 80 ÷ 8 = | 56 ÷ 8 = | 8 ÷ 8 = | 32 ÷ 8 = |
| 56 ÷ 8 = | 72 ÷ 8 = | 16 ÷ 8 = | 40 ÷ 8 = |
| Score | Score | Score | Score |

# Adding two-digit numbers to multiples of 10

See if you can answer each set of 20 questions in one minute.

| | | | |
|---|---|---|---|
| 80 + 26 = | 70 + 21 = | 50 + 21 = | 60 + 44 = |
| 30 + 47 = | 60 + 34 = | 60 + 34 = | 20 + 56 = |
| 70 + 33 = | 20 + 59 = | 20 + 45 = | 40 + 31 = |
| 50 + 43 = | 30 + 66 = | 40 + 18 = | 80 + 29 = |
| 60 + 12 = | 50 + 24 = | 10 + 58 = | 50 + 53 = |
| 20 + 45 = | 70 + 15 = | 60 + 33 = | 30 + 66 = |
| 60 + 56 = | 60 + 38 = | 50 + 12 = | 10 + 84 = |
| 40 + 19 = | 20 + 46 = | 60 + 63 = | 60 + 41 = |
| 50 + 23 = | 60 + 55 = | 20 + 88 = | 40 + 33 = |
| 80 + 15 = | 30 + 49 = | 70 + 42 = | 30 + 74 = |
| 20 + 74 = | 40 + 53 = | 90 + 24 = | 50 + 39 = |
| 30 + 56 = | 50 + 21 = | 60 + 72 = | 70 + 21 = |
| 10 + 68 = | 40 + 64 = | 30 + 11 = | 80 + 11 = |
| 50 + 42 = | 30 + 78 = | 90 + 53 = | 90 + 26 = |
| 60 + 14 = | 20 + 81 = | 40 + 27 = | 50 + 44 = |
| 80 + 35 = | 40 + 34 = | 50 + 46 = | 60 + 25 = |
| 90 + 26 = | 50 + 44 = | 30 + 82 = | 80 + 33 = |
| 40 + 44 = | 60 + 16 = | 60 + 75 = | 40 + 67 = |
| 50 + 31 = | 50 + 28 = | 80 + 33 = | 30 + 54 = |
| 30 + 63 = | 40 + 52 = | 20 + 66 = | 70 + 22 = |
| Score | Score | Score | Score |

For answers see page 31

# The 9 times table

 See if you can answer each set of 20 questions in one minute.

|  |  |  |  |
|---|---|---|---|
| 0 x 9 = | 9 x 9 = | 9 x 9 = | 1 x 9 = |
| 1 x 9 = | 8 x 9 = | 2 x 9 = | 6 x 9 = |
| 2 x 9 = | 5 x 9 = | 4 x 9 = | 5 x 9 = |
| 3 x 9 = | 0 x 9 = | 5 x 9 = | 4 x 9 = |
| 4 x 9 = | 4 x 9 = | 8 x 9 = | 8 x 9 = |
| 5 x 9 = | 3 x 9 = | 6 x 9 = | 7 x 9 = |
| 6 x 9 = | 1 x 9 = | 3 x 9 = | 10 x 9 = |
| 7 x 9 = | 10 x 9 = | 1 x 9 = | 0 x 9 = |
| 8 x 9 = | 6 x 9 = | 0 x 9 = | 3 x 9 = |
| 9 x 9 = | 7 x 9 = | 7 x 9 = | 9 x 9 = |
| 10 x 9 = | 2 x 9 = | 10 x 9 = | 2 x 9 = |
| 90 ÷ 9 = | 90 ÷ 9 = | 54 ÷ 9 = | 72 ÷ 9 = |
| 45 ÷ 9 = | 27 ÷ 9 = | 90 ÷ 9 = | 63 ÷ 9 = |
| 9 ÷ 9 = | 45 ÷ 9 = | 81 ÷ 9 = | 18 ÷ 9 = |
| 72 ÷ 9 = | 9 ÷ 9 = | 63 ÷ 9 = | 27 ÷ 9 = |
| 54 ÷ 9 = | 72 ÷ 9 = | 9 ÷ 9 = | 90 ÷ 9 = |
| 27 ÷ 9 = | 54 ÷ 9 = | 72 ÷ 9 = | 9 ÷ 9 = |
| 18 ÷ 9 = | 18 ÷ 9 = | 45 ÷ 9 = | 54 ÷ 9 = |
| 36 ÷ 9 = | 63 ÷ 9 = | 18 ÷ 9 = | 36 ÷ 9 = |
| 63 ÷ 9 = | 36 ÷ 9 = | 36 ÷ 9 = | 45 ÷ 9 = |
| Score | Score | Score | Score |

# Subtracting two-digit numbers from multiples of 10

See if you can answer each set of 20 questions in one minute.

| | | | |
|---|---|---|---|
| 60 − 23 = | 90 − 54 = | 40 − 29 = | 40 − 21 = |
| 90 − 71 = | 80 − 61 = | 30 − 15 = | 50 − 35 = |
| 80 − 48 = | 40 − 22 = | 50 − 37 = | 60 − 43 = |
| 50 − 19 = | 70 − 19 = | 20 − 13 = | 70 − 28 = |
| 40 − 32 = | 50 − 36 = | 60 − 44 = | 80 − 37 = |
| 20 − 13 = | 60 − 21 = | 70 − 15 = | 20 − 14 = |
| 70 − 45 = | 30 − 18 = | 80 − 56 = | 30 − 27 = |
| 50 − 39 = | 20 − 13 = | 90 − 64 = | 40 − 22 = |
| 70 − 21 = | 80 − 55 = | 50 − 32 = | 50 − 36 = |
| 60 − 34 = | 70 − 27 = | 40 − 14 = | 60 − 25 = |
| 40 − 18 = | 50 − 38 = | 20 − 15 = | 70 − 52 = |
| 30 − 25 = | 60 − 44 = | 60 − 35 = | 80 − 44 = |
| 80 − 65 = | 40 − 29 = | 70 − 62 = | 40 − 38 = |
| 50 − 41 = | 30 − 18 = | 80 − 53 = | 30 − 17 = |
| 90 − 44 = | 20 − 11 = | 50 − 36 = | 60 − 42 = |
| 50 − 22 = | 80 − 45 = | 70 − 31 = | 70 − 53 = |
| 40 − 36 = | 90 − 63 = | 80 − 42 = | 80 − 66 = |
| 80 − 21 = | 70 − 47 = | 60 − 41 = | 90 − 61 = |
| 70 − 52 = | 60 − 33 = | 80 − 25 = | 50 − 37 = |
| 60 − 34 = | 50 − 24 = | 60 − 42 = | 40 − 17 = |
| Score | Score | Score | Score |

For answers see page 31

# Multiplying by 10

See if you can answer each set of 20 questions in one minute.

| | |
|---|---|
| 10 × 7 = 70 | 10 × 46 = 460 |
| 36 × 10 = 360 | 28 × 10 = 280 |
| 10 × 48 = 480 | 36 × 10 = 360 |
| 4 × 10 = 40 | 10 × 24 = 240 |
| 10 × 56 = 560 | 51 × 10 = 510 |
| 10 × 22 = 220 | 10 × 36 = 360 |
| 8 × 10 = 80 | 10 × 48 = 480 |
| 52 × 10 = 520 | 74 × 10 = 740 |
| 10 × 67 = 670 | 53 × 10 = 530 |
| 26 × 10 = 260 | 10 × 9 = 90 |
| 10 × 55 = 550 | 44 × 10 = 440 |
| 53 × 10 = 530 | 64 × 10 = 640 |
| 19 × 10 = 190 | 32 × 10 = 320 |
| 10 × 63 = 630 | 10 × 16 = 160 |
| 41 × 10 = 40 | 10 × 52 = 520 |
| 10 × 58 = 580 | 34 × 10 = 340 |
| 37 × 10 = 370 | 10 × 63 = 630 |
| 6 × 10 = 60 | 58 × 10 = 580 |
| 19 × 10 = 190 | 10 × 33 = 330 |
| 10 × 25 = 250 | 47 × 10 = 470 |

Score ____

Score ____

| | |
|---|---|
| 29 × 10 = 290 | 10 × 31 = 310 |
| 36 × 10 = 360 | 8 × 10 = 80 |
| 10 × 42 = 420 | 17 × 10 = 170 |
| 10 × 31 = 310 | 10 × 26 = 260 |
| 4 × 10 = 40 | 63 × 10 = 630 |
| 10 × 39 = 390 | 10 × 44 = 440 |
| 46 × 10 = 460 | 58 × 10 = 580 |
| 10 × 24 = 240 | 10 × 35 = 350 |
| 58 × 10 = 580 | 10 × 41 = 410 |
| 10 × 35 = 350 | 66 × 10 = 660 |
| 63 × 10 = 630 | 10 × 72 = 720 |
| 95 × 10 = 950 | 89 × 10 = 890 |
| 10 × 85 = 850 | 96 × 10 = 960 |
| 44 × 10 = 440 | 38 × 10 = 380 |
| 7 × 10 = 70 | 10 × 47 = 101  470 |
| 10 × 25 = 250 | 10 × 25 = 250 |
| 37 × 10 = 370 | 29 × 10 = 290 |
| 10 × 18 = 180 | 10 × 53 = 530 |
| 93 × 10 = 930 | 48 × 10 = 480 |
| 10 × 76 = 760 | 10 × 38 = 380 |

Score ____

Score ____

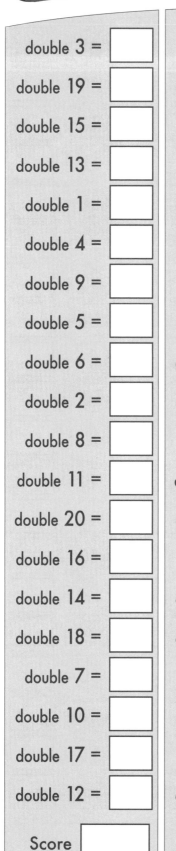

# Finding doubles of numbers from 1 to 20

See if you can answer each set of 20 questions in one minute.

| | | | |
|---|---|---|---|
| double 3 = | double 6 = | double 14 = | double 15 = |
| double 19 = | double 18 = | double 9 = | double 2 = |
| double 15 = | double 1 = | double 2 = | double 9 = |
| double 13 = | double 5 = | double 17 = | double 16 = |
| double 1 = | double 13 = | double 6 = | double 11 = |
| double 4 = | double 17 = | double 3 = | double 6 = |
| double 9 = | double 2 = | double 8 = | double 3 = |
| double 5 = | double 7 = | double 19 = | double 18 = |
| double 6 = | double 10 = | double 10 = | double 5 = |
| double 2 = | double 14 = | double 20 = | double 20 = |
| double 8 = | double 3 = | double 15 = | double 13 = |
| double 11 = | double 20 = | double 1 = | double 4 = |
| double 20 = | double 16 = | double 4 = | double 17 = |
| double 16 = | double 4 = | double 12 = | double 10 = |
| double 14 = | double 19 = | double 7 = | double 19 = |
| double 18 = | double 15 = | double 16 = | double 8 = |
| double 7 = | double 8 = | double 5 = | double 7 = |
| double 10 = | double 11 = | double 11 = | double 14 = |
| double 17 = | double 9 = | double 13 = | double 12 = |
| double 12 = | double 12 = | double 18 = | double 1 = |
| Score | Score | Score | Score |

# Finding doubles of numbers from 1 to 50

See if you can answer each set of 20 questions in one minute.

| | | | |
|---|---|---|---|
| double 5 = | double 48 = | double 6 = | double 8 = |
| double 44 = | double 36 = | double 27 = | double 27 = |
| double 26 = | double 27 = | double 44 = | double 31 = |
| double 31 = | double 8 = | double 1 = | double 45 = |
| double 49 = | double 14 = | double 34 = | double 11 = |
| double 12 = | double 25 = | double 21 = | double 16 = |
| double 18 = | double 17 = | double 18 = | double 28 = |
| double 21 = | double 9 = | double 39 = | double 49 = |
| double 33 = | double 33 = | double 40 = | double 13 = |
| double 29 = | double 21 = | double 28 = | double 10 = |
| double 46 = | double 40 = | double 9 = | double 2 = |
| double 19 = | double 18 = | double 11 = | double 22 = |
| double 16 = | double 5 = | double 15 = | double 35 = |
| double 11 = | double 10 = | double 4 = | double 5 = |
| double 13 = | double 28 = | double 23 = | double 25 = |
| double 1 = | double 19 = | double 36 = | double 39 = |
| double 6 = | double 1 = | double 47 = | double 24 = |
| double 30 = | double 41 = | double 30 = | double 4 = |
| double 9 = | double 16 = | double 12 = | double 12 = |
| double 41 = | double 3 = | double 7 = | double 18 = |
| Score | Score | Score | Score |

# Finding doubles of numbers from 51 to 100

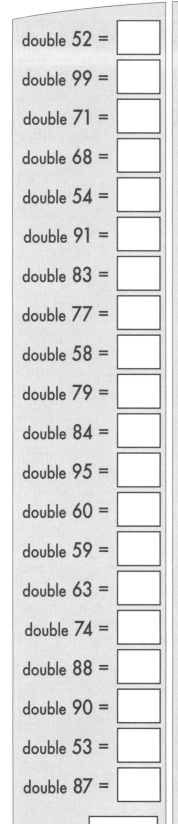

See if you can answer each set of 20 questions in one minute.

| | | | |
|---|---|---|---|
| double 52 = | double 51 = | double 55 = | double 81 = |
| double 99 = | double 72 = | double 61 = | double 76 = |
| double 71 = | double 89 = | double 88 = | double 52 = |
| double 68 = | double 64 = | double 53 = | double 98 = |
| double 54 = | double 91 = | double 77 = | double 77 = |
| double 91 = | double 58 = | double 81 = | double 55 = |
| double 83 = | double 93 = | double 62 = | double 83 = |
| double 77 = | double 78 = | double 96 = | double 70 = |
| double 58 = | double 55 = | double 79 = | double 85 = |
| double 79 = | double 60 = | double 83 = | double 92 = |
| double 84 = | double 81 = | double 56 = | double 62 = |
| double 95 = | double 95 = | double 66 = | double 51 = |
| double 60 = | double 82 = | double 94 = | double 64 = |
| double 59 = | double 76 = | double 71 = | double 73 = |
| double 63 = | double 57 = | double 58 = | double 89 = |
| double 74 = | double 69 = | double 72 = | double 10 = |
| double 88 = | double 84 = | double 52 = | double 71 = |
| double 90 = | double 73 = | double 90 = | double 96 = |
| double 53 = | double 67 = | double 73 = | double 57 = |
| double 87 = | double 80 = | double 84 = | double 84 = |
| Score | Score | Score | Score |

For answers see page 32

# Finding 50% of even numbers to 100

See if you can answer each set of 20 questions in one minute.

| | | | |
|---|---|---|---|
| 50% of 4 = | 50% of 44 = | 50% of 18 = | 50% of 8 = |
| 50% of 88 = | 50% of 8 = | 50% of 28 = | 50% of 92 = |
| 50% of 42 = | 50% of 98 = | 50% of 34 = | 50% of 72 = |
| 50% of 68 = | 50% of 30 = | 50% of 56 = | 50% of 44 = |
| 50% of 34 = | 50% of 54 = | 50% of 92 = | 50% of 36 = |
| 50% of 70 = | 50% of 76 = | 50% of 66 = | 50% of 86 = |
| 50% of 10 = | 50% of 82 = | 50% of 74 = | 50% of 68 = |
| 50% of 52 = | 50% of 40 = | 50% of 60 = | 50% of 12 = |
| 50% of 62 = | 50% of 86 = | 50% of 38 = | 50% of 94 = |
| 50% of 38 = | 50% of 38 = | 50% of 4 = | 50% of 56 = |
| 50% of 50 = | 50% of 26 = | 50% of 84 = | 50% of 16 = |
| 50% of 26 = | 50% of 14 = | 50% of 24 = | 50% of 30 = |
| 50% of 18 = | 50% of 70 = | 50% of 46 = | 50% of 48 = |
| 50% of 6 = | 50% of 34 = | 50% of 68 = | 50% of 74 = |
| 50% of 96 = | 50% of 48 = | 50% of 78 = | 50% of 80 = |
| 50% of 74 = | 50% of 50 = | 50% of 14 = | 50% of 62 = |
| 50% of 32 = | 50% of 42 = | 50% of 52 = | 50% of 2 = |
| 50% of 48 = | 50% of 36 = | 50% of 86 = | 50% of 34 = |
| 50% of 58 = | 50% of 60 = | 50% of 98 = | 50% of 54 = |
| 50% of 76 = | 50% of 72 = | 50% of 30 = | 50% of 20 = |
| Score | Score | Score | Score |

# Finding 50% of odd numbers to 99

See if you can answer each set of 20 questions in one minute.

| | | | |
|---|---|---|---|
| 50% of 99 = | 50% of 35 = | 50% of 33 = | 50% of 63 = |
| 50% of 31 = | 50% of 17 = | 50% of 97 = | 50% of 41 = |
| 50% of 49 = | 50% of 49 = | 50% of 41 = | 50% of 57 = |
| 50% of 57 = | 50% of 71 = | 50% of 55 = | 50% of 95 = |
| 50% of 69 = | 50% of 95 = | 50% of 69 = | 50% of 39 = |
| 50% of 45 = | 50% of 55 = | 50% of 99 = | 50% of 71 = |
| 50% of 81 = | 50% of 69 = | 50% of 43 = | 50% of 97 = |
| 50% of 93 = | 50% of 93 = | 50% of 57 = | 50% of 35 = |
| 50% of 21 = | 50% of 41 = | 50% of 61 = | 50% of 83 = |
| 50% of 17 = | 50% of 37 = | 50% of 5 = | 50% of 97 = |
| 50% of 75 = | 50% of 21 = | 50% of 21 = | 50% of 67 = |
| 50% of 89 = | 50% of 9 = | 50% of 77 = | 50% of 75 = |
| 50% of 41 = | 50% of 53 = | 50% of 63 = | 50% of 19 = |
| 50% of 33 = | 50% of 67 = | 50% of 85 = | 50% of 9 = |
| 50% of 51 = | 50% of 81 = | 50% of 27 = | 50% of 81 = |
| 50% of 19 = | 50% of 59 = | 50% of 49 = | 50% of 23 = |
| 50% of 3 = | 50% of 3 = | 50% of 51 = | 50% of 77 = |
| 50% of 77 = | 50% of 27 = | 50% of 37 = | 50% of 65 = |
| 50% of 39 = | 50% of 85 = | 50% of 81 = | 50% of 49 = |
| 50% of 55 = | 50% of 91 = | 50% of 65 = | 50% of 53 = |
| Score | Score | Score | Score |

For answers see page 32

# Adding decimals

See if you can answer each set of 20 questions in one minute.

| | | | |
|---|---|---|---|
| 0.6 + 0.7 = | 0.4 + 0.4 = | 1.2 + 0.5 = | 1.2 + 0.5 = |
| 0.3 + 1.5 = | 1.1 + 0.6 = | 0.3 + 0.7 = | 0.9 + 0.3 = |
| 0.9 + 0.2 = | 0.9 + 0.3 = | 0.6 + 0.8 = | 1.2 + 0.4 = |
| 1.4 + 0.5 = | 1.2 + 0.6 = | 0.9 + 0.1 = | 1.1 + 0.5 = |
| 1.1 + 0.7 = | 0.7 + 0.7 = | 0.6 + 0.6 = | 0.1 + 0.2 = |
| 0.5 + 0.5 = | 0.8 + 0.4 = | 0.7 + 0.1 = | 0.5 + 0.7 = |
| 0.6 + 0.3 = | 0.9 + 0.6 = | 0.2 + 0.3 = | 0.3 + 0.6 = |
| 1.0 + 0.1 = | 1.4 + 0.5 = | 0.4 + 1.1 = | 0.6 + 0.5 = |
| 0.4 + 0.9 = | 1.3 + 0.1 = | 1.0 + 0.6 = | 0.7 + 0.7 = |
| 0.1 + 1.7 = | 0.8 + 1.0 = | 0.8 + 0.8 = | 1.1 + 0.3 = |
| 0.3 + 0.8 = | 0.4 + 0.7 = | 1.1 + 0.1 = | 1.5 + 0.1 = |
| 0.5 + 0.8 = | 0.6 + 1.1 = | 0.1 + 1.6 = | 0.4 + 0.1 = |
| 0.4 + 0.1 = | 1.3 + 0.5 = | 1.5 + 0.3 = | 0.6 + 0.6 = |
| 0.5 + 0.6 = | 0.5 + 0.6 = | 0.9 + 0.3 = | 0.2 + 0.4 = |
| 1.2 + 0.3 = | 0.3 + 1.1 = | 0.2 + 0.5 = | 1.4 + 0.3 = |
| 1.8 + 0.1 = | 1.4 + 0.3 = | 1.2 + 0.3 = | 0.6 + 0.2 = |
| 0.9 + 0.9 = | 0.8 + 0.2 = | 0.8 + 0.2 = | 0.2 + 0.3 = |
| 1.3 + 0.4 = | 0.1 + 0.3 = | 0.2 + 1.4 = | 0.7 + 0.4 = |
| 0.7 + 0.5 = | 1.4 + 0.9 = | 0.5 + 1.3 = | 0.2 + 0.6 = |
| 0.2 + 1.9 = | 0.3 + 1.2 = | 0.9 + 0.2 = | 0.5 + 0.3 = |
| Score | Score | Score | Score |

# Subtracting decimals

See if you can answer each set of 20 questions in one minute.

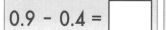

| | | | |
|---|---|---|---|
| 0.9 − 0.4 = | 1.3 − 0.1 = | 1.9 − 0.3 = | 1.2 − 0.8 = |
| 1.7 − 0.7 = | 0.8 − 0.1 = | 1.4 − 0.7 = | 0.9 − 0.8 = |
| 0.8 − 0.3 = | 0.4 − 0.2 = | 2 − 1.3 = | 0.6 − 0.3 = |
| 0.8 − 0.5 = | 2 − 0.3 = | 0.9 − 0.7 = | 1.1 − 0.3 = |
| 0.4 − 0.1 = | 1.9 − 0.1 = | 1.1 − 1.0 = | 1.7 − 0.5 = |
| 0.6 − 0.5 = | 0.7 − 0.3 = | 0.5 − 0.4 = | 1.8 − 0.3 = |
| 1.2 − 0.3 = | 0.5 − 0.2 = | 1.5 − 0.3 = | 1.5 − 0.4 = |
| 1.8 − 0.1 = | 0.3 − 0.1 = | 0.8 − 0.6 = | 0.7 − 0.4 = |
| 0.9 − 0.2 = | 1.1 − 0.8 = | 0.7 − 0.1 = | 2 − 1.5 = |
| 1.3 − 0.4 = | 1.5 − 0.3 = | 0.5 − 0.2 = | 1.9 − 1.7 = |
| 0.7 − 0.5 = | 1.3 − 0.9 = | 1.1 − 0.5 = | 1.5 − 0.3 = |
| 2 − 1.9 = | 1.8 − 1.2 = | 1.2 − 0.8 = | 1.7 − 1.1 = |
| 0.4 − 0.2 = | 1.5 − 0.7 = | 1.3 − 0.4 = | 1.8 − 1.2 = |
| 1.1 − 0.6 = | 0.9 − 0.3 = | 1.6 − 0.1 = | 0.8 − 0.5 = |
| 0.9 − 0.3 = | 0.5 − 0.3 = | 1.8 − 0.3 = | 0.3 − 0.1 = |
| 1.2 − 0.6 = | 0.4 − 0.1 = | 0.7 − 0.2 = | 1.1 − 0.8 = |
| 0.8 − 0.4 = | 1.2 − 0.8 = | 1.9 − 1.6 = | 0.4 − 0.2 = |
| 0.9 − 0.6 = | 1.5 − 0.6 = | 1.2 − 0.7 = | 1 − 0.5 = |
| 1.4 − 0.5 = | 1.1 − 0.4 = | 1.5 − 1.2 = | 1.3 − 0.4 = |
| 0.7 − 0.5 = | 1.2 − 0.6 = | 1 − 0.6 = | 1.9 − 0.1 = |
| Score | Score | Score | Score |

For answers see page 32

# Mental maths mixture

See if you can answer each set of 20 questions in one minute.

| | | | |
|---|---|---|---|
| 7 + 9 = | 4 x 7 = | 2 x 5 = | quarter of 28 = |
| 5 x 9 = | double 13 = | half of 13 = | 7 + 15 = |
| quarter of 8 = | 50% of 25 = | 72 ÷ 9 = | 5 x 2 = |
| 12 ÷ 2 = | 12 + 13 = | double 51 = | 50% of 62 = |
| 0.7 + 0.4 = | 9 x 2 = | 52 – 5 = | 18 ÷ 3 = |
| 10 x 4 = | quarter of 20 = | 50% of 78 = | 1.0 + 0.4 = |
| 19 – 6 = | 1.3 – 0.5 = | 10 x 49 = | half of 27 = |
| 36 x 10 = | 25 – 7 = | 70 + 34 = | 49 ÷ 7 = |
| half of 56 = | 45 ÷ 5 = | 24 ÷ 6 = | 10 x 14 = |
| 12 + 4 = | 60 + 28 = | 0 x 9 = | 0.9 – 0.3 = |
| 6 x 8 = | 5 x 6 = | 0.3 + 1.4 = | 20 ÷ 5 = |
| 50% of 12 = | 16 + 13 = | double 14 = | 50% of 46 = |
| 70 + 34 = | half of 63 = | 7 x 4 = | quarter of 36 = |
| 6 x 3 = | 64 ÷ 8 = | 1.7 – 1.2 = | 1.9 – 0.7 = |
| quarter of 16 = | 10 x 31 = | half of 25 = | 40 + 34 = |
| 1.1 – 0.6 = | 0.4 + 1.1 = | 56 ÷ 8 = | 27 ÷ 3 = |
| 17 + 3 = | 50 – 13 = | quarter of 44 = | 6 x 4 = |
| 2 x 5 = | double 34 = | 53 x 10 = | 16 x 10 = |
| 50% of 36 = | 6 x 7 = | 8 x 3 = | double 23 = |
| double 43 = | half of 26 = | 66 + 3 = | 5 x 2 = |
| Score | Score | Score | Score |

For answers see page 32

## Page 3
### Adding numbers up to 30

| Column 1 | Column 2 | Column 3 | Column 4 |
|---|---|---|---|
| 16 | 25 | 27 | 29 |
| 25 | 21 | 24 | 26 |
| 20 | 23 | 21 | 26 |
| 13 | 29 | 21 | 24 |
| 21 | 21 | 23 | 27 |
| 24 | 21 | 15 | 28 |
| 15 | 30 | 19 | 28 |
| 24 | 21 | 22 | 22 |
| 16 | 24 | 27 | 29 |
| 22 | 24 | 27 | 23 |
| 24 | 28 | 21 | 16 |
| 28 | 30 | 13 | 24 |
| 11 | 27 | 29 | 20 |
| 28 | 21 | 22 | 28 |
| 21 | 17 | 29 | 21 |
| 24 | 22 | 22 | 22 |
| 20 | 27 | 22 | 25 |
| 9 | 26 | 10 | 27 |
| 15 | 27 | 20 | 25 |
| 16 | 29 | 19 | 26 |

## Page 4
### Subtracting numbers up to 30

| Column 1 | Column 2 | Column 3 | Column 4 |
|---|---|---|---|
| 18 | 14 | 6 | 11 |
| 8 | 17 | 16 | 16 |
| 13 | 13 | 12 | 6 |
| 12 | 14 | 6 | 2 |
| 6 | 9 | 2 | 12 |
| 19 | 14 | 11 | 7 |
| 5 | 21 | 8 | 4 |
| 8 | 18 | 8 | 3 |
| 13 | 5 | 9 | 0 |
| 5 | 7 | 3 | 6 |
| 7 | 15 | 12 | 7 |
| 5 | 23 | 4 | 5 |
| 2 | 5 | 24 | 7 |
| 4 | 2 | 11 | 4 |
| 12 | 17 | 5 | 4 |
| 16 | 6 | 6 | 3 |
| 2 | 8 | 8 | 3 |
| 13 | 21 | 5 | 12 |
| 9 | 12 | 4 | 6 |
| 11 | 14 | 6 | 13 |

## Page 5
### Addition and subtraction up to 30

| Column 1 | Column 2 | Column 3 | Column 4 |
|---|---|---|---|
| 28 | 26 | 13 | 11 |
| 16 | 6 | 24 | 28 |
| 12 | 24 | 8 | 12 |
| 29 | 12 | 13 | 24 |
| 4 | 24 | 2 | 11 |
| 22 | 24 | 11 | 22 |
| 29 | 5 | 7 | 8 |
| 6 | 21 | 12 | 6 |
| 21 | 15 | 24 | 24 |
| 18 | 14 | 3 | 4 |
| 21 | 16 | 24 | 15 |
| 8 | 12 | 6 | 28 |
| 27 | 27 | 13 | 5 |
| 28 | 27 | 5 | 16 |
| 3 | 21 | 19 | 21 |
| 30 | 22 | 20 | 3 |
| 18 | 4 | 13 | 29 |
| 21 | 21 | 21 | 7 |
| 2 | 16 | 17 | 22 |
| 25 | 23 | 23 | 9 |

## Page 6
### The 2 times table

| Column 1 | Column 2 | Column 3 | Column 4 |
|---|---|---|---|
| 0 | 8 | 12 | 16 |
| 2 | 16 | 16 | 6 |
| 4 | 0 | 4 | 0 |
| 6 | 20 | 20 | 20 |
| 8 | 12 | 2 | 18 |
| 10 | 4 | 10 | 10 |
| 12 | 18 | 0 | 14 |
| 14 | 6 | 6 | 4 |
| 16 | 2 | 8 | 8 |
| 18 | 10 | 14 | 2 |
| 20 | 14 | 18 | 12 |
| 9 | 8 | 6 | 10 |
| 5 | 1 | 3 | 9 |
| 2 | 6 | 2 | 1 |
| 3 | 10 | 5 | 4 |
| 7 | 3 | 1 | 2 |
| 4 | 2 | 4 | 5 |
| 1 | 9 | 9 | 7 |
| 10 | 4 | 8 | 3 |
| 8 | 7 | 7 | 8 |

## Page 7
### The 3 times table

| Column 1 | Column 2 | Column 3 | Column 4 |
|---|---|---|---|
| 0 | 15 | 12 | 24 |
| 3 | 24 | 3 | 6 |
| 6 | 30 | 27 | 27 |
| 9 | 6 | 15 | 0 |
| 12 | 18 | 18 | 18 |
| 15 | 21 | 30 | 3 |
| 18 | 27 | 24 | 12 |
| 21 | 0 | 6 | 30 |
| 24 | 12 | 0 | 9 |
| 27 | 3 | 21 | 15 |
| 30 | 9 | 9 | 21 |
| 8 | 8 | 10 | 5 |
| 5 | 5 | 8 | 9 |
| 6 | 3 | 1 | 2 |
| 3 | 1 | 5 | 1 |
| 10 | 10 | 3 | 4 |
| 2 | 7 | 2 | 10 |
| 4 | 2 | 6 | 8 |
| 9 | 9 | 4 | 6 |
| 1 | 6 | 7 | 6 |

## Page 8
### Adding one-digit numbers to two-digit numbers

| Column 1 | Column 2 | Column 3 | Column 4 |
|---|---|---|---|
| 65 | 51 | 81 | 25 |
| 31 | 73 | 72 | 51 |
| 76 | 41 | 34 | 66 |
| 81 | 32 | 51 | 41 |
| 65 | 61 | 44 | 73 |
| 91 | 91 | 54 | 51 |
| 41 | 91 | 31 | 71 |
| 51 | 43 | 61 | 81 |
| 72 | 51 | 74 | 64 |
| 81 | 64 | 42 | 41 |
| 62 | 31 | 96 | 41 |
| 91 | 72 | 61 | 31 |
| 33 | 31 | 82 | 22 |
| 71 | 21 | 22 | 81 |
| 91 | 34 | 31 | 52 |
| 31 | 64 | 43 | 85 |
| 22 | 72 | 51 | 31 |
| 74 | 31 | 72 | 71 |
| 41 | 93 | 91 | 61 |
| 23 | 45 | 32 | 42 |

## Page 9
### The 4 times table

| Column 1 | Column 2 | Column 3 | Column 4 |
|---|---|---|---|
| 0 | 16 | 36 | 8 |
| 4 | 0 | 4 | 28 |
| 8 | 28 | 12 | 40 |
| 12 | 20 | 24 | 12 |
| 16 | 40 | 20 | 4 |
| 20 | 32 | 16 | 24 |
| 24 | 4 | 0 | 36 |
| 28 | 12 | 40 | 20 |
| 32 | 36 | 8 | 32 |
| 36 | 8 | 32 | 16 |
| 40 | 24 | 28 | 0 |
| 9 | 1 | 5 | 10 |
| 3 | 4 | 7 | 3 |
| 2 | 6 | 4 | 1 |
| 10 | 8 | 2 | 9 |
| 8 | 10 | 6 | 2 |
| 4 | 2 | 1 | 6 |
| 1 | 7 | 10 | 4 |
| 6 | 9 | 9 | 7 |
| 5 | 5 | 8 | 5 |

## Page 10
### Subtracting one-digit numbers from two-digit numbers

| Column 1 | Column 2 | Column 3 | Column 4 |
|---|---|---|---|
| 86 | 49 | 58 | 14 |
| 73 | 37 | 29 | 57 |
| 67 | 77 | 68 | 39 |
| 47 | 56 | 37 | 78 |
| 5 | 69 | 69 | 66 |
| 24 | 19 | 29 | 86 |
| 38 | 58 | 36 | 54 |
| 49 | 25 | 47 | 18 |
| 79 | 79 | 79 | 37 |
| 68 | 35 | 47 | 69 |
| 28 | 48 | 37 | 49 |
| 58 | 18 | 25 | 29 |
| 66 | 76 | 59 | 19 |
| 27 | 69 | 65 | 54 |
| 38 | 76 | 36 | 79 |
| 54 | 38 | 57 | 39 |
| 38 | 66 | 66 | 59 |
| 17 | 79 | 29 | 68 |
| 25 | 19 | 18 | 29 |
| 25 | 37 | 59 | 47 |

## Page 11
### The 5 times table

| Column 1 | Column 2 | Column 3 | Column 4 |
|---|---|---|---|
| 0 | 10 | 35 | 0 |
| 5 | 30 | 0 | 40 |
| 10 | 45 | 20 | 25 |
| 15 | 50 | 5 | 15 |
| 20 | 0 | 45 | 5 |
| 25 | 15 | 25 | 50 |
| 30 | 40 | 15 | 10 |
| 35 | 20 | 30 | 20 |
| 40 | 5 | 50 | 30 |
| 45 | 25 | 40 | 45 |
| 50 | 35 | 10 | 35 |
| 8 | 10 | 2 | 1 |
| 4 | 6 | 7 | 3 |
| 1 | 9 | 5 | 10 |
| 3 | 5 | 4 | 5 |
| 10 | 2 | 8 | 6 |
| 9 | 1 | 10 | 2 |
| 2 | 3 | 1 | 8 |
| 7 | 7 | 6 | 4 |
| 6 | 4 | 9 | 9 |

**Answers**

## Page 12
### Finding halves of even numbers

| Column 1 | Column 2 | Column 3 | Column 4 |
|---|---|---|---|
| 24 | 36 | 37 | 18 |
| 35 | 17 | 44 | 12 |
| 12 | 44 | 32 | 24 |
| 6 | 23 | 14 | 25 |
| 17 | 29 | 26 | 16 |
| 33 | 11 | 17 | 47 |
| 26 | 24 | 11 | 32 |
| 32 | 49 | 8 | 44 |
| 9 | 38 | 39 | 15 |
| 37 | 21 | 47 | 21 |
| 21 | 26 | 23 | 31 |
| 43 | 18 | 29 | 27 |
| 18 | 33 | 5 | 22 |
| 29 | 7 | 12 | 43 |
| 34 | 32 | 42 | 19 |
| 7 | 27 | 22 | 5 |
| 23 | 48 | 26 | 33 |
| 25 | 30 | 20 | 42 |
| 11 | 19 | 28 | 48 |
| 20 | 9 | 47 | 26 |

## Page 13
### The 6 times table

| Column 1 | Column 2 | Column 3 | Column 4 |
|---|---|---|---|
| 0 | 12 | 30 | 6 |
| 6 | 42 | 6 | 54 |
| 12 | 0 | 60 | 24 |
| 18 | 60 | 48 | 12 |
| 24 | 18 | 24 | 30 |
| 30 | 24 | 18 | 42 |
| 36 | 54 | 54 | 0 |
| 42 | 6 | 36 | 18 |
| 48 | 30 | 12 | 48 |
| 54 | 48 | 0 | 60 |
| 60 | 36 | 42 | 36 |
| 8 | 10 | 1 | 9 |
| 10 | 7 | 6 | 7 |
| 2 | 4 | 8 | 2 |
| 5 | 3 | 10 | 5 |
| 1 | 1 | 7 | 10 |
| 7 | 5 | 5 | 3 |
| 4 | 8 | 9 | 6 |
| 3 | 2 | 4 | 1 |
| 9 | 6 | 3 | 8 |

## Page 14
### Finding halves of odd numbers

| Column 1 | Column 2 | Column 3 | Column 4 |
|---|---|---|---|
| 8½ | 38½ | 1½ | 42½ |
| 20½ | 43½ | 28½ | 23½ |
| 3½ | 10½ | 36½ | 5½ |
| 11½ | 13½ | 45½ | 21½ |
| 47½ | 24½ | 37½ | 48½ |
| 27½ | 31½ | 7½ | 8½ |
| 39½ | 18½ | 32½ | 9½ |
| 9½ | 26½ | 25½ | 13½ |
| 41½ | 35½ | 6½ | 33½ |
| 2½ | 12½ | 40½ | 29½ |
| 49½ | 16½ | 12½ | 36½ |
| 23½ | 14½ | 17½ | 15½ |
| 42½ | 34½ | 44½ | 31½ |
| 22½ | 29½ | 19½ | 3½ |
| 15½ | 10½ | 9½ | 4½ |

## Page 15
### The 7 times table

| Column 1 | Column 2 | Column 3 | Column 4 |
|---|---|---|---|
| 0 | 14 | 35 | 28 |
| 7 | 35 | 63 | 7 |
| 14 | 63 | 0 | 70 |
| 21 | 0 | 28 | 14 |
| 28 | 42 | 14 | 63 |
| 35 | 21 | 42 | 49 |
| 42 | 7 | 7 | 21 |
| 49 | 70 | 21 | 0 |
| 56 | 56 | 70 | 35 |
| 63 | 28 | 49 | 56 |
| 70 | 49 | 56 | 42 |
| 7 | 2 | 6 | 10 |
| 6 | 4 | 9 | 5 |
| 8 | 1 | 1 | 8 |
| 1 | 10 | 5 | 2 |
| 5 | 8 | 7 | 7 |
| 10 | 3 | 2 | 3 |
| 4 | 5 | 10 | 6 |
| 3 | 6 | 8 | 1 |
| 2 | 7 | 4 | 4 |

## Page 16
### Finding quarters

| Column 1 | Column 2 | Column 3 | Column 4 |
|---|---|---|---|
| 3 | 5 | 4 | 6 |
| 22 | 4 | 20 | 2 |
| 15 | 11 | 6 | 11 |
| 9 | 17 | 8 | 7 |
| 10 | 2 | 14 | 10 |
| 8 | 21 | 18 | 25 |
| 16 | 25 | 2 | 16 |
| 4 | 10 | 7 | 3 |
| 1 | 6 | 9 | 21 |
| 5 | 22 | 1 | 19 |
| 14 | 9 | 3 | 12 |
| 21 | 7 | 10 | 15 |
| 6 | 3 | 2 | 3 |
| 7 | 12 | 15 | 4 |
| 13 | 18 | 5 | 5 |

## Page 17
### The 8 times table

| Column 1 | Column 2 | Column 3 | Column 4 |
|---|---|---|---|
| 0 | 16 | 40 | 72 |
| 8 | 80 | 24 | 16 |
| 16 | 24 | 8 | 40 |
| 24 | 56 | 48 | 80 |
| 32 | 48 | 0 | 24 |
| 40 | 32 | 32 | 8 |
| 48 | 72 | 64 | 32 |
| 56 | 8 | 16 | 64 |
| 64 | 64 | 80 | 0 |
| 72 | 0 | 56 | 48 |
| 80 | 40 | 72 | 56 |
| 8 | 1 | 4 | 8 |
| 1 | 5 | 10 | 2 |
| 2 | 10 | 7 | 7 |
| 5 | 3 | 5 | 1 |
| 3 | 4 | 6 | 10 |
| 9 | 6 | 9 | 3 |
| 10 | 7 | 1 | 4 |
| 7 | 9 | 2 | 5 |

## Page 18
### Adding two-digit numbers to multiples of 10

| Column 1 | Column 2 | Column 3 | Column 4 |
|---|---|---|---|
| 106 | 91 | 71 | 104 |
| 77 | 94 | 94 | 76 |
| 103 | 79 | 65 | 71 |
| 93 | 96 | 58 | 109 |
| 72 | 74 | 68 | 103 |
| 65 | 85 | 93 | 96 |
| 116 | 98 | 62 | 94 |
| 59 | 66 | 123 | 101 |
| 73 | 115 | 108 | 73 |
| 95 | 79 | 112 | 104 |
| 94 | 93 | 114 | 89 |
| 86 | 71 | 132 | 91 |
| 78 | 104 | 41 | 91 |
| 92 | 108 | 143 | 116 |
| 74 | 101 | 67 | 94 |
| 115 | 74 | 96 | 85 |
| 116 | 94 | 112 | 113 |
| 84 | 76 | 135 | 107 |
| 81 | 78 | 113 | 84 |
| 93 | 92 | 86 | 92 |

## Page 19
### The 9 times table

| Column 1 | Column 2 | Column 3 | Column 4 |
|---|---|---|---|
| 0 | 81 | 81 | 9 |
| 9 | 72 | 18 | 54 |
| 18 | 45 | 36 | 45 |
| 27 | 0 | 45 | 36 |
| 36 | 36 | 72 | 72 |
| 45 | 27 | 54 | 63 |
| 54 | 9 | 27 | 90 |
| 63 | 90 | 9 | 0 |
| 72 | 54 | 0 | 27 |
| 81 | 63 | 63 | 81 |
| 90 | 18 | 90 | 18 |
| 10 | 10 | 6 | 8 |
| 5 | 3 | 10 | 7 |
| 1 | 5 | 9 | 2 |
| 8 | 1 | 7 | 3 |
| 6 | 8 | 1 | 10 |
| 3 | 6 | 8 | 1 |
| 2 | 2 | 5 | 6 |
| 4 | 7 | 2 | 4 |
| 7 | 4 | 4 | 5 |

## Page 20
### Subtracting two-digit numbers from multiples of 10

| Column 1 | Column 2 | Column 3 | Column 4 |
|---|---|---|---|
| 37 | 36 | 11 | 19 |
| 19 | 19 | 15 | 15 |
| 32 | 18 | 13 | 17 |
| 31 | 51 | 7 | 42 |
| 8 | 14 | 16 | 43 |
| 7 | 39 | 55 | 6 |
| 25 | 12 | 24 | 3 |
| 11 | 7 | 26 | 18 |
| 49 | 25 | 18 | 14 |
| 26 | 43 | 26 | 35 |
| 22 | 12 | 5 | 18 |
| 5 | 16 | 25 | 36 |
| 15 | 11 | 8 | 2 |
| 9 | 12 | 27 | 13 |
| 46 | 9 | 14 | 18 |
| 28 | 35 | 39 | 17 |
| 4 | 27 | 38 | 14 |
| 59 | 23 | 19 | 29 |
| 26 | 26 | 18 | 23 |

**Answers** 31

## Page 21
### Multiplying by 10

| Column 1 | Column 2 | Column 3 | Column 4 |
| --- | --- | --- | --- |
| 70 | 460 | 290 | 310 |
| 360 | 280 | 360 | 80 |
| 480 | 360 | 420 | 170 |
| 40 | 240 | 310 | 260 |
| 560 | 510 | 40 | 630 |
| 220 | 360 | 390 | 440 |
| 80 | 480 | 460 | 580 |
| 520 | 740 | 240 | 350 |
| 670 | 530 | 580 | 410 |
| 260 | 90 | 350 | 660 |
| 550 | 440 | 630 | 720 |
| 530 | 640 | 950 | 890 |
| 190 | 320 | 850 | 960 |
| 630 | 160 | 440 | 380 |
| 410 | 520 | 70 | 470 |
| 580 | 340 | 250 | 250 |
| 370 | 630 | 370 | 290 |
| 60 | 580 | 180 | 530 |
| 190 | 330 | 930 | 480 |
| 250 | 470 | 760 | 380 |

## Page 22
### Finding doubles of numbers from 1 to 20

| Column 1 | Column 2 | Column 3 | Column 4 |
| --- | --- | --- | --- |
| 6 | 12 | 28 | 30 |
| 38 | 36 | 18 | 4 |
| 30 | 2 | 4 | 18 |
| 26 | 10 | 34 | 32 |
| 2 | 26 | 12 | 22 |
| 8 | 34 | 6 | 12 |
| 18 | 4 | 16 | 6 |
| 10 | 14 | 38 | 36 |
| 12 | 20 | 20 | 10 |
| 4 | 28 | 40 | 40 |
| 16 | 6 | 30 | 26 |
| 22 | 40 | 2 | 8 |
| 40 | 32 | 8 | 34 |
| 32 | 8 | 24 | 20 |
| 28 | 38 | 14 | 38 |
| 36 | 30 | 32 | 16 |
| 14 | 16 | 10 | 14 |
| 20 | 22 | 22 | 28 |
| 34 | 18 | 26 | 24 |
| 24 | 24 | 36 | 2 |

## Page 23
### Finding doubles of numbers from 1 to 50

| Column 1 | Column 2 | Column 3 | Column 4 |
| --- | --- | --- | --- |
| 10 | 96 | 12 | 16 |
| 88 | 72 | 54 | 54 |
| 52 | 54 | 88 | 62 |
| 62 | 16 | 2 | 90 |
| 98 | 28 | 68 | 22 |
| 24 | 50 | 42 | 32 |
| 36 | 34 | 36 | 56 |
| 42 | 18 | 78 | 98 |
| 66 | 66 | 80 | 26 |
| 58 | 42 | 56 | 20 |
| 92 | 80 | 18 | 4 |
| 38 | 36 | 22 | 44 |
| 32 | 10 | 30 | 70 |
| 22 | 20 | 8 | 10 |
| 26 | 56 | 46 | 50 |
| 2 | 38 | 72 | 78 |
| 12 | 2 | 94 | 48 |
| 60 | 82 | 60 | 8 |
| 18 | 32 | 24 | 24 |
| 82 | 6 | 14 | 36 |

## Page 24
### Finding doubles of numbers from 51 to 100

| Column 1 | Column 2 | Column 3 | Column 4 |
| --- | --- | --- | --- |
| 104 | 102 | 110 | 162 |
| 198 | 144 | 122 | 152 |
| 142 | 178 | 176 | 104 |
| 136 | 128 | 106 | 196 |
| 108 | 182 | 154 | 154 |
| 182 | 116 | 162 | 110 |
| 166 | 186 | 124 | 166 |
| 154 | 156 | 192 | 140 |
| 116 | 110 | 158 | 170 |
| 158 | 120 | 166 | 184 |
| 168 | 162 | 112 | 124 |
| 190 | 190 | 132 | 102 |
| 120 | 164 | 188 | 128 |
| 118 | 152 | 142 | 146 |
| 126 | 114 | 116 | 178 |
| 148 | 138 | 144 | 20 |
| 176 | 168 | 104 | 142 |
| 180 | 146 | 180 | 192 |
| 106 | 134 | 146 | 114 |
| 174 | 160 | 168 | 168 |

## Page 25
### Finding 50% of even numbers to 100

| Column 1 | Column 2 | Column 3 | Column 4 |
| --- | --- | --- | --- |
| 2 | 22 | 9 | 4 |
| 44 | 4 | 14 | 46 |
| 21 | 49 | 17 | 36 |
| 34 | 15 | 28 | 22 |
| 17 | 27 | 46 | 18 |
| 35 | 38 | 33 | 43 |
| 5 | 41 | 37 | 34 |
| 26 | 20 | 30 | 6 |
| 31 | 43 | 19 | 47 |
| 19 | 19 | 2 | 28 |
| 25 | 13 | 42 | 8 |
| 13 | 7 | 12 | 15 |
| 9 | 35 | 23 | 24 |
| 3 | 17 | 34 | 37 |
| 48 | 24 | 39 | 40 |
| 37 | 25 | 7 | 31 |
| 16 | 21 | 26 | 1 |
| 24 | 18 | 43 | 17 |
| 29 | 30 | 49 | 27 |
| 38 | 36 | 15 | 10 |

## Page 26
### Finding 50% of odd numbers to 99

| Column 1 | Column 2 | Column 3 | Column 4 |
| --- | --- | --- | --- |
| 49.5 | 17.5 | 16.5 | 31.5 |
| 15.5 | 8.5 | 48.5 | 20.5 |
| 24.5 | 24.5 | 20.5 | 28.5 |
| 28.5 | 35.5 | 27.5 | 47.5 |
| 34.5 | 47.5 | 34.5 | 19.5 |
| 22.5 | 27.5 | 49.5 | 35.5 |
| 40.5 | 34.5 | 21.5 | 48.5 |
| 46.5 | 46.5 | 28.5 | 17.5 |
| 10.5 | 20.5 | 30.5 | 41.5 |
| 8.5 | 18.5 | 2.5 | 48.5 |
| 37.5 | 10.5 | 10.5 | 33.5 |
| 44.5 | 4.5 | 38.5 | 37.5 |
| 20.5 | 26.5 | 31.5 | 9.5 |
| 16.5 | 33.5 | 42.5 | 4.5 |
| 25.5 | 40.5 | 13.5 | 40.5 |
| 9.5 | 29.5 | 24.5 | 11.5 |
| 1.5 | 1.5 | 25.5 | 38.5 |
| 38.5 | 13.5 | 18.5 | 32.5 |
| 19.5 | 42.5 | 40.5 | 24.5 |
| 27.5 | 45.5 | 32.5 | 26.5 |

## Page 27
### Adding decimals

| Column 1 | Column 2 | Column 3 | Column 4 |
| --- | --- | --- | --- |
| 1.3 | 0.8 | 1.7 | 1.7 |
| 1.8 | 1.7 | 1 | 1.2 |
| 1.1 | 1.2 | 1.4 | 1.6 |
| 1.9 | 1.8 | 1 | 1.6 |
| 1.8 | 1.4 | 1.2 | 0.3 |
| 1 | 1.2 | 0.8 | 1.2 |
| 0.9 | 1.5 | 0.5 | 0.9 |
| 1.1 | 1.9 | 1.5 | 1.1 |
| 1.3 | 1.4 | 1.6 | 1.4 |
| 1.8 | 1.8 | 1.6 | 1.4 |
| 1.1 | 1.1 | 1.2 | 1.6 |
| 1.3 | 1.7 | 1.7 | 0.5 |
| 0.5 | 1.8 | 1.8 | 1.2 |
| 1.1 | 1.1 | 1.2 | 0.6 |
| 1.5 | 1.4 | 0.7 | 1.7 |
| 1.9 | 1.7 | 1.5 | 0.8 |
| 1.8 | 1 | 1 | 0.5 |
| 1.7 | 0.4 | 1.6 | 1.1 |
| 1.2 | 2.3 | 1.8 | 0.8 |
| 2.1 | 1.5 | 1.1 | 0.8 |

## Page 28
### Subtracting decimals

| Column 1 | Column 2 | Column 3 | Column 4 |
| --- | --- | --- | --- |
| 0.5 | 1.2 | 1.6 | 0.4 |
| 1 | 0.7 | 0.7 | 0.1 |
| 0.5 | 0.2 | 0.7 | 0.3 |
| 0.3 | 1.7 | 0.2 | 0.8 |
| 0.3 | 1.8 | 0.1 | 1.2 |
| 0.1 | 0.4 | 0.1 | 1.5 |
| 0.9 | 0.3 | 1.2 | 1.1 |
| 1.7 | 0.2 | 0.2 | 0.3 |
| 0.7 | 0.3 | 0.6 | 0.5 |
| 0.9 | 1.2 | 0.3 | 0.2 |
| 0.2 | 0.4 | 0.6 | 1.2 |
| 0.1 | 0.6 | 0.4 | 0.6 |
| 0.2 | 0.8 | 0.9 | 0.6 |
| 0.5 | 0.6 | 1.5 | 0.3 |
| 0.6 | 0.2 | 1.5 | 0.2 |
| 0.4 | 0.4 | 0.3 | 0.2 |
| 0.3 | 0.9 | 0.5 | 0.5 |
| 0.9 | 0.7 | 0.3 | 0.9 |
| 0.2 | 0.6 | 0.4 | 1.8 |

## Page 29
### Mental maths mixture

| Column 1 | Column 2 | Column 3 | Column 4 |
| --- | --- | --- | --- |
| 16 | 28 | 10 | 7 |
| 45 | 26 | 6.5 | 22 |
| 2 | 12.5 | 8 | 10 |
| 6 | 25 | 102 | 31 |
| 1.1 | 18 | 47 | 6 |
| 40 | 5 | 39 | 1.5 |
| 13 | 0.8 | 490 | 13.5 |
| 360 | 18 | 104 | 7 |
| 28 | 9 | 4 | 140 |
| 16 | 88 | 0 | 0.6 |
| 48 | 30 | 1.7 | 4 |
| 6 | 29 | 28 | 23 |
| 104 | 31.5 | 28 | 9 |
| 18 | 8 | 0.5 | 1.2 |
| 4 | 310 | 12.5 | 74 |
| 0.5 | 1.5 | 7 | 9 |
| 20 | 37 | 11 | 24 |
| 10 | 68 | 530 | 160 |
| 18 | 42 | 24 | 46 |
| 86 | 13 | 69 | 10 |